Anna E. Richter

Oil in Iraq

How to overcome the Resource Curse?

Anchor Compact

Richter, Anna: Oil in Iraq: How to overcome the Resource Curse? Hamburg, Anchor Academic Publishing 2014

Buch-ISBN: 978-3-95489-318-8
PDF-eBook-ISBN: 978-3-95489-818-3
Druck/Herstellung: Anchor Academic Publishing, Hamburg, 2014

Bibliografische Information der Deutschen Nationalbibliothek:
Die Deutsche Nationalbibliothek verzeichnet diese Publikation in der Deutschen Nationalbibliografie; detaillierte bibliografische Daten sind im Internet über http://dnb.d-nb.de abrufbar

Bibliographical Information of the German National Library:
The German National Library lists this publication in the German National Bibliography. Detailed bibliographic data can be found at: http://dnb.d-nb.de

© Anchor Academic Publishing, ein Imprint der Diplomica® Verlag GmbH
http://www.diplom.de, Hamburg 2014
Printed in Germany

Table of contents

Introduction

This paper will have a closer look at the overwhelming importance of non-renewable resources for the Iraqi economy and how the profits made by oil exports should be invested to ensure the best possible outcome, in order to finally overcome "the resource curse". As found by economic analysis and sector assessments: *"Iraq's economic, poverty and conflict future will be largely determined by the government's ability to govern the economy in the transparent and better use of oil revenues and establishment of wealth redistribution mechanisms."*[1]

In the first chapter the risks for any economy stemming from resource abundance will be assessed, then in section 1.2. the specific challenges for Iraq. In the second chapter, we will have a look at the Macroeconomic environment and specifically at the current oil sector in Iraq in section 2.2.

Finally in the third chapter the recommended steps towards a more inclusive growth path that serves both government and wider societal interests (jobs, transparency, accountability and inclusive growth) will be outlined.

---

[1] United States Agency - International Development. (2012). USAID-TIJARA PROVINCIAL ECONOMIC GROWTH PROGRAM. New York: Report for Prime Minister's Advisory Commission (PMAC). p.1

Chapter 1: Resource Curse

1.1. Definition and implications

The so called "resource curse" is a widely used term describing the phenomenon that often countries with oil or other natural resource wealth experience slower economic growth. What seems like an counter-intuitive statement at first, was proven widely in a large number of studies.[2] [3] There are several hypothesis to explain how resource abundance is a threat to economic growth:

- most oil producers are price-takers and therefore vulnerable to price-fluctuation. Saudi-Arabia stands out to certain extend, due to its large size in world oil markets. However the assumption generally proves right, especially taking into account the diminishing monopoly of OPEC and its low success in binding its members to their assigned quotas.[4]
- Oil wealth can hit non-oil exports as a result of exchange rate valuation.
- An increased budget allows the government to employ more civil servants, to strengthen political support. Oil rich states often find themselves with an exorbitant, inefficient public sector.[5]
- The perspective of Oil wealth can be subject to the whims of various groups leading to structural imbalances, which could potentially fuel further conflict.[6]

---

[2] For a large sum of such studies see: Frankel, J. (2010). The Natural Resource Curse: A Survey. HKS Faculty Research Working Paper Series, p.1-45.

[3] Bjorvatn, K., Farzanegan, M. R., & Schneider, F. (2012, 7 0). Resource Curse and Power Balance: Evidence from Oil-Rich Countries. *World Development, 40*, 1308--1316.

[4] For more details see: Frankel, J. (2010). The Natural Resource Curse: A Survey. HKS Faculty Research Working Paper Series, p.5

[5] Humphreys, M., Sachs, J., & Stiglitz, J. E. (Eds.). (2007). Escaping the resource curse (pp. 11-13). New York: Columbia University Press. p.207

[6] Kjetil Bjorvatn, Mohammad Reza Farzanegan, Friedrich Schneider, Resource Curse and Power Balance: Evidence from Oil-Rich Countries, World Development, Volume 40, Issue 7, July 2012, Pages 1308-1316, ISSN 0305-750X, http://dx.doi.org/10.1016/j.worlddev.2012.03.003.

Several recent papers suggest that the negative association between natural resource intensity and economic growth can be reversed if institutional quality is high enough.[7] Therefore the resource curse should not be interpreted as a rule that resource-rich countries are doomed to failure, but rather be perceived as a double-edged sword, with both benefits and dangers. In countries with sufficiently good institutions resource dependency may instead contribute positively to economic growth.[8]

1.2. The Resource Curse in Iraq

Iraqi oil reserves are among the largest of the world (143 Million barrels).[9][10] In the 1970's Iraq had reached middle income status, and possessed in regional comparison, a high quality education and healthcare system, as well as a modern infrastructure. World oil prices were high, and Iraq's oil production rose from 1.5 million barrels per day in 1970 to 3.5 million bpd in 1979.[11] Soaring oil revenues allowed the government to investment into non-oil-related sectors so that both, the oil and non-oil sectors grew rapidly.[12]

With the beginning of the Iran-Iraq war 1980, oil production almost ceased overnight. Production levels averaged at 1 million barrels per day 1981-1985. With Gulf War I in 1990 Oil production stagnated

---

[7] Boschini, A., Pettersson, J., & Roine, J. (2013, 3 0). The Resource Curse and its Potential Reversal. World Development, 43, 19--41.

[8] For more detail see: Mehlum, H., Moene, K., & Torvik, R. (2006). Institutions and the resource curse. The Economic Journal, 116(508), 1-20.

[9] Talal A. Al-Kassar & Jared S. Soileau (2014) New development: Accounting and accountability for government revenues in Iraq, Public Money & Management, 34:1, p. 67, DOI: 10.1080/09540962.2014.865944

[10] According to some papers, second largest oil reserves in the world after Saudi-Arabia: Talal A. Al-Kassar & Jared S. Soileau (2014) New development: Accounting and accountability for government revenues in Iraq, Public Money & Management, 34:1, p. 67, DOI: 10.1080/09540962.2014.865944 , others say third behind Saudi Arabia and Canada: Mausner, Loi, Cordesman "Iraq's Coming National Challenges: Developing the Petroleum Sector." Center for Strategic and International Studies, January 5, 2011.

[11] Foote, C., Block, W., Crane, K., & Gray, S. (2004-08-01T00:00:00). Economic Policy and Prospects in Iraq. The Journal of Economic Perspectives, 18, pp.47-70.

[12] Foote, C., Block, W., Crane, K., & Gray, S. (2004-08-01T00:00:00). Economic Policy and Prospects in Iraq. The Journal of Economic Perspectives, 18, p.49

entirely once again.[13] After the war, exports were constrained by an United Nations embargo. Oil production did not exceed the national consumption level until 1996 when Iraq agreed to the Oil-for-Food program, which allowed Iraq to export oil for humanitarian supplies from 1997 until 2003.[14]

TOTAL OIL PRODUCTION IN IRAQ

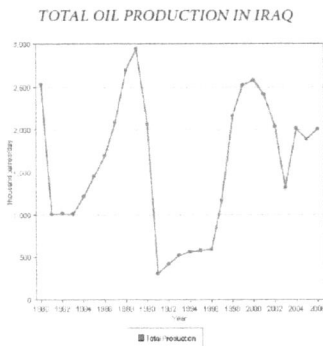

US Energy Information Administration, January 1, 2010   15

Shattering wars, inefficient economic and financial policies and international sanctions impaired previous social and economic gains and damaged political institutions. The GDP per capita has fallen from US$3400 in 1980 to less than US$800 in 2004.[16]

While in 1993 more than 50% of total state revenue stemmed from taxation since 2008 taxation does not provide for more than 3%. As seen in the table below in 2013 97% of total revenue derives from other sources, including oil and gas revenue.

---

[13] Foote, C., Block, W., Crane, K., & Gray, S. (2004-08-01T00:00:00). Economic Policy and Prospects in Iraq. The Journal of Economic Perspectives, 18, p.49

[14] Iraq was accused of underpricing the oil to attract bribes. To read more about this controversy see: Hsieh, C.-T., & Moretti, E. (2006). Did Iraq Cheat the United Nations? Underpricing, Bribes, and the Oil for Food Program. The Quarterly Journal of Economics, 121, p. 1211-1248.

[15] Donovan, T. W. (2010). Iraq's Petroleum Industry: Unsettled Issues. Washington D.C.: Middle East Institute.p.20

[16] Talal A. Al-Kassar & Jared S. Soileau (2014) New development: Accounting and accountability for government revenues in Iraq, Public Money & Management, 34:1, p. 67, DOI: 10.1080/09540962.2014.865944

Table 1. Tax revenue in Iraq as a percentage of total revenue.

	Tax revenue as a percentage of GDP	Revenue sources as percentage of total revenue			
		Direct taxes	Indirect taxes	Trade taxes	Others (including oil revenue)
Developing countries (average) *	18.5	29.7	28.1	27.6	14.6
Iraq (1993)**	2.3	40.5	9.7	0	49.8
Iraq (2008)***	7.0	0.66	0.37	0	98.97
Iraq (2012)***	5.0	2.0	0.5	0	97.5
Iraq (2013)***	5.5	2.1	0.6	0	97.3

Sources: *ASOSAI (2010).
** Supreme Audit Board (1994).
*** Ministry of Finance and Ministry of Planning (2009; 2012; 2013).

17

Stated employed Iraqis were exempted from taxation prior to 2005.[18] The decreasing percentage of tax revenue as a percentage of total state revenue further illustrates the high dependency on oil exports. Moreover when citizens are not expected to pay for government services, there is little tax bargain, to hold the government accountable.[19]

Oil-price fluctuation can harm the Iraqi economy drastically. It becomes clear that channeling the revenues of non-renewable resources in a way to promote non-oil based growth is a massive challenge of utmost importance.

Due to the phenomenon of the so called "resource curse", as explained above, the high dependency of non-renewable-energy exports, threatens a democratic development of Iraq. The major comparative advantage of Iraq and the crucial element for a potential sustainable development, might itself be an impediment to broad-based (equitable) economic growth.

---

[17] Talal A. Al-Kassar & Jared S. Soileau (2014) New development: Accounting and accountability for government revenues in Iraq, Public Money & Management, 34:1, p. 68, DOI: 10.1080/09540962.2014.865944

[18] Ibid. p.67

[19] An alternative would be to transfer oil revenues directly to citizens, which would then be taxed to finance public expenditures. The argument is that spending that is financed by taxation accruing directly to the government—is more likely to be scrutinized by citizens and hence subject to greater efficiency. For more information see: Devarajan, Shantayanan and Raballand, Gaël and Le, Tuan Minh, Direct Redistribution, Taxation, and Accountability in Oil-Rich Economies: A Proposal (December 20, 2011). Center for Global Development Working Paper No. 281. Available at
SRN: http://ssrn.com/abstract=2009385 or http://dx.doi.org/10.2139/ssrn.2009385

The challenge for the Iraqi government therefore will be to learn from the successes and failures of other countries, which found themselves in similar situations.

The US Aid report on Iraq states frankly: *"Unfortunately, (...) Iraq's resource wealth not only remains a threat to its democracy, it also stands as a potential impediment to sustainable growth. Iraq is therefore at a crossroads, with a largely dysfunctional economic framework short-circuiting necessary investment, which leads to gross imbalances and inefficiencies.*[20]

---

[20] United States Agency - International Development. (2012). *USAID-TIJARA PROVINCIAL ECONOMIC GROWTH PROGRAM.* New York: Report for Prime Minister's Advisory Commission (PMAC). p.1

Chapter 2: Economic environment

2.1. The current economic environment

The current Iraqi economy is primarily based on two sectors. The Oil and Gas sector which accounts for almost 60% of GDP, but characteristically only employs about 1% of workforce, and the public sector, accounting for 10% of GDP while employing a 3rd of the workforce.

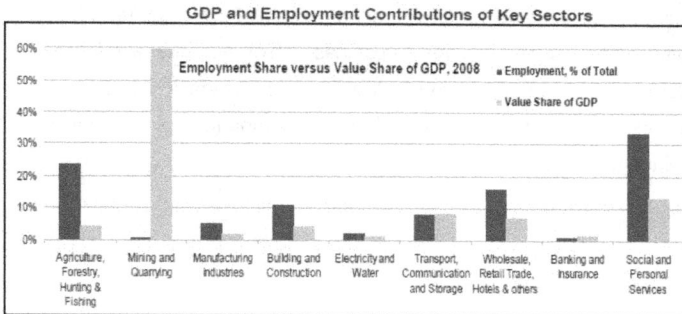

GDP and Employment Contributions of Key Sectors

[21]

2.2. The Oil Sector

Iraq is estimated to have the third largest oil reserves in the world after Saudi-Arabia and Iran. The concrete number given is 115 billion barrels. The US Department of Energy Information Administration criticizes however, that the above estimate relies on data from three decades ago and has not been revised since 2001.[22] Further reserves are expected to be discovered. Estimations however vary between 45 and 99 billion barrels.[23]

---

[21] United States Agency - International Development. (2012). *USAID-TIJARA PROVINCIAL ECONOMIC GROWTH PROGRAM.* New York: Report for Prime Minister's Advisory Commission (PMAC). p.42

[22] US Energy Information Administration. (2009). Country Analysis Brief: Iraq. Washington.

[23] Blanchard, C. M. (2010). Iraq: Oil and Gas Sector, Revenue Sharing and U.S. Policy. Washington: Congressional Research Service. p.1

65% of Iraq's currently proven Oil reserves are located in the south, particularly in the governorate of Al Basrah. Large proven oil resources also are located in the northern governorate of Al Tamim near the disputed city of Kirkuk.[24]

There are 28 giant fields in Iraq, which hold an estimated 12% of the entire proven global reserves. Four of these fields are among the largest fields in the world.[25]

The Iraqi Oil Ministry started offering service contracts to international oil companies in June 2009. More than 80% of Oil reserves of the bidding parties were Chinese corporates, which are now the largest investor and consumer in Iraq.[26] A weak and unclear legal status of investors prevented many international oil companies to take part in the bidding process.

---

[24] Blanchard, C. M. (2010). Iraq: Oil and Gas Sector, Revenue Sharing and U.S. Policy. Washington: Congressional Research Service. p.1

[25] Donovan, T. W. (2010). Iraq's Petroleum Industry: Unsettled Issues. Washington D.C.: Middle East Institute.p.6

[26] Donovan, T. W. (2010). Iraq's Petroleum Industry: Unsettled Issues. Washington D.C.: Middle East Institute.p.6-7

Congressional Research Service, October 1, 2008   27

The semi-autonomous status of the Kurdistan region further fuels the uncertainty if investments in Iraq will be secure and contracts between Kurdistan Region and the Iraqi Government are largely ambiguous in language.[28]

By setting the production goals unrealistically high, expectations of Iraqis were risen and will most likely be disappointed.

The discontent among the population in some oil-rich regions in Iraq rose further, after it became clear that the Chinese corporations employed barely any local workers. Oil-rich regions and regions with few or non-oil reserves equally feel that they deserve a higher share in oil revenue. Another issue, of utmost relevance are the different ethnic / religious groups Sunnis, Shia and Kurds are not satisfied with the current outcome.[29]

---

[28] Donovan, T. W. (2010). Iraq's Petroleum Industry: Unsettled Issues. Washington D.C.: Middle East Institute.p.7

[29] Donovan, T. W. (2010). Iraq's Petroleum Industry: Unsettled Issues. Washington D.C.: Middle East Institute.p.10

Chapter 3: Recommended Steps

3.1. Distribution of Power

In a state where Government Revenue is so heavily dependent on Oil, as in Iraq, whoever controls Oil, controls the country.

The Iraqi constitution states that Iraq's natural resources are the property of *"all the people of Iraq in all regions and governorates,"* and that *"the federal government, with the producing governorates and regional governments, shall undertake the management of oil and gas extracted from present fields."*[30]

The 2005 Constitution envisions a federal Iraq that divides power between a federal government, state-level governates and the semi-autonomous Kurdish region—a balance of power that would prevent a return to dictatorship, with no individual or faction having a monopoly control of Iraq's oil.

Since the last election and the formation of the Maliki-led coalition government, a strong Kurdish regional government has evolved alongside a dysfunctional and increasingly autocratic federal government in Baghdad. The governates, seeing the benefits that autonomy has brought the Kurds, want it for themselves, or at least a larger share of oil revenues.

Therefore competencies about oil revenue must be distributed clearly and fairly, which of course will be extremely hard to achieve.

Keith Myers, a London based oil analyst of Iraq Revenue Watch, finds it:" hard to imagine a resolution of the current legal and regulatory vacuum anytime soon. It may take a new government and an amended Constitution, or even a new generation of leaders, decades down the line, to fix the problems of Iraq's post-dictator oil power structure. This is a lesson for the countries of the Arab Spring."[31]

---

[30] UNHCR, Constitution of Iraq. Article 111 and 112. For an unofficial English Translation of the Iraqi Constitution see: http://www.refworld.org/pdfid/454f50804.pdf

[31] Myers, K. (2012, May 9). Iraq Revenue Watch. Retrieved May 14, 2014, from Oil, Power and Democracy in Iraq: Can They Be Reconciled?: http://www.iraqrevenuewatch.org/news/oil-power-and-democracy-iraq-can-they-be-reconciled

3.2. Inclusive not-oil growth

Iraq now is at a crossroad, and seriously needs to peruse an consistent strategy to diversify its economy. The government has to provide opportunities for inclusive non-oil growth. Using oil revenues as an enabling resource, will be critical to future success.[32]

3.1.1. Investment in Infrastructure and Human Capital

Maintaining the infrastructure is essential to attract foreign investment and to create entrepreneurial incentive within the country. Currently electricity supply only meets 50 percent of consumer demand, transportation networks need to be reformed, water supply and sanitation infrastructure are run down, and other critical public services such as the provision of education and health services are inadequate to meet the needs of a growing population and modern economy.

The Iraqi Government will have to institute major reforms, and invest in physical infrastructure and human capital to create a more attractive business environment.[33]

3.1.2. Develop the private sector

Public payrolls consume government revenues, which are very much needed to invest in infrastructure, communications, electricity supply, water and sanitation, schools, and public health.

The public sector is too large and despite the recognition of the problem, the public sector keeps on growing.[34] Since 2005, according to federal budgets the size of government workforce increased from

---

[32] United States Agency - International Development. (2012). *USAID-TIJARA PROVINCIAL ECONOMIC GROWTH PROGRAM.* New York: Report for Prime Minister's Advisory Commission (PMAC). p.2

[33] United States Agency - International Development. (2012). *USAID-TIJARA PROVINCIAL ECONOMIC GROWTH PROGRAM.* New York: Report for Prime Minister's Advisory Commission (PMAC).p.96

[34] United States Agency - International Development. (2012). USAID-TIJARA PROVINCIAL ECONOMIC GROWTH PROGRAM. New York: Report for Prime Minister's Advisory Commission (PMAC).p. 32

1,2 million to 2,3 million.[35] With every new public sector employee, the long term recurrent costs and pension liabilities undermine future growth. Recent incentives of the Iraqi government eroded the private sector further, for example by mandating state sector enterprises to deal in the first instance only with other state sector enterprises.[36]

Most state employees are low-skilled and would face difficulties finding work in the private sector. This might explain the discrepancies between the National Development Plan and the actual policies of the Iraqi government.[37] In the absence of alternative workplaces the government of Iraq does has been sustaining the economy as it always has: by employing people in the public sector! Furthermore almost half of the Iraqi population would be most inclined to support a party that created mote government jobs.

Political Attitudes of Iraqis

"I would be more likely to support a party that advocated or promised . . ."

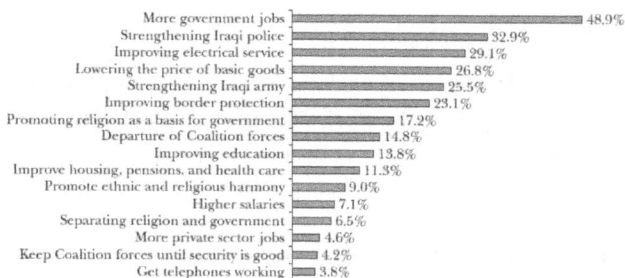

More government jobs	48.9%
Strengthening Iraqi police	32.9%
Improving electrical service	29.1%
Lowering the price of basic goods	26.8%
Strengthening Iraqi army	25.5%
Improving border protection	23.1%
Promoting religion as a basis for government	17.2%
Departure of Coalition forces	14.8%
Improving education	13.8%
Improve housing, pensions, and health care	11.3%
Promote ethnic and religious harmony	9.0%
Higher salaries	7.1%
Separating religion and government	6.5%
More private sector jobs	4.6%
Keep Coalition forces until security is good	4.2%
Get telephones working	3.8%

38

[35] Robertson, C. (2008, August 10). The New York Times. Retrieved April 23, 2014, from Iraq Private Sector Falters; Rolls of Government Soar: http://www.nytimes.com/2008/08/11/world/middleeast/11baghdad.html?pagewanted=all

[36] United States Agency - International Development. (2012). USAID-TIJARA PROVINCIAL ECONOMIC GROWTH PROGRAM. New York: Report for Prime Minister's Advisory Commission (PMAC).p. 33

[37] United States Agency - International Development. (2012). USAID-TIJARA PROVINCIAL ECONOMIC GROWTH PROGRAM. New York: Report for Prime Minister's Advisory Commission (PMAC).p.38

[38] Foote, C., Block, W., Crane, K., & Gray, S. (2004). Economic policy and prospects in Iraq. The Journal of Economic Perspectives, 18, p.69

To escape this vicious circle a variety of incentives are needed, facilitating making business and access to loans.

3.1.3. Facilitate Making Business

It is of utmost importance to create incentives for private investors by creating more transparent and efficient mechanisms to issue permits and licenses.[39]

In the Doing Business Report 2014, a yearly study published by the World Bank, which measures the costs to small and medium enterprises (SMEs) of business regulations in 189 countries, Iraq sits on place 151. In the past 5 years only 7 economies did not implement any changes to facilitate business for SMEs. Iraq is one of them.[40]

According to a joint study of the United Nations and the World Bank the main obstacles to private-sector investment were poor access to finance, telecommunication problems, macroeconomic instability and street crime.[41]

A poll found that 96 percent of Iraqis believed that violence would decrease if more employment opportunities were created. However violence is also one of the main obstacles for job creation, which leaves us with a tragic chicken-egg dilemma.[42]

3.1.4. Reopening Banks and Encouraging Lending

Besides the two main state banks Rafidain and Rasheed, private banks started to emerge after 2000.[43] However the crucial section of loans, especially for small and medium sized enterprises developed

---

[39] United States Agency for International Development. (2012). PROVINCIAL ECONOMIC GROWTH PROGRAM - IRAQ. Washington. p. 46

[40] World Bank Group. (2014). Doing Business Report 2014. Washington D.C.: World Bank Group. p. 11

[41] United Nations, World Bank. (2003). Joint Iraq Needs Assessment: Investment Climate. New York: UN.

[42] Oxford Research International. (2004). National Survey of Iraq: February 2004. Oxford.

[43] Foote, C., Block, W., Crane, K., & Gray, S. (2004-08-01T00:00:00). Economic Policy and Prospects in Iraq. The Journal of Economic Perspectives, 18, p.62.

slowly. 12 banks have established SME lending units by 2012.[44] The public increasingly uses this possibility. While in 2010 only ~5% of registered SMEs enjoyed bank financing, the number rose significantly after, as illustrated in the table below.[45]

USAID-*TIJARA* PARTNER BANK SME LOANS BY YEAR

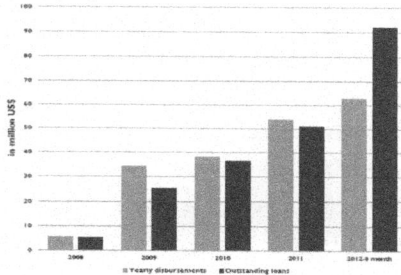

[46]

3.2. Oil related policies

3.2.1. Nationwide Revenue Sharing

A transparent and fair policy on revenue distribution must be implemented. Clear national hydrocarbon laws must be issued, also addressing the issue, of possible government changes. National hydrocarbon laws should reach by consensus among all major stakeholders, Arabs and Kurds, Sunnis and Shi'as, all the governates the oil-rich and the ones without natural resources.[47]

3.2.2. Foreign Investment

There are several ways to structure the national oil industry. First of all the **concession system** in charge before the nationalization 1661 and 1972, in which the government granted foreign companies

[44] United States Agency for International Development. (2012). PROVINCIAL ECONOMIC GROWTH PROGRAM - IRAQ. Washington. p. 11

[45] United States Agency for International Development. (2012). PROVINCIAL ECONOMIC GROWTH PROGRAM - IRAQ. Washington. p. 11

[46] United States Agency for International Development. (2012). PROVINCIAL ECONOMIC GROWTH PROGRAM - IRAQ. Washington. p. 12

[47] Donovan, T. W. (2010). Iraq's Petroleum Industry: Unsettled Issues. Washington D.C.: Middle East Institute.p.14

licenses to extract oil, which then remains in the property of the foreign company. The government receives taxes.[48]

A second system was in place from 1970 to 2009. The **oil industry was nationalized** and oil remains in the hand of the state.[49] Ibrahim Bahr al Uloum, Oil Minister of Iraq at the time stated in 2003 that National Oil Companies *"no longer serve the best interest of their countries. Rather, … their inherent inefficiencies, born of their protection from competitive forces endowed by their monopoly status, cost the countries in which they survive billions of dollars."[50] A variance of this option is currently in place:* Technical Service Agreements in which the state remains in control of the oil and reimbursed the production company.[51]

The third option are **Production Sharing Agreements**. The state technically remains in charge of the oil, while a foreign company extracts it under contract. The foreign corporation arranges for the capital investment, construction and infrastructure. Profits are shared between the state and the corporation in agreed proportions. The corporation may also be taxed on its profits.[52]

Several scholars argue that Iraq should not rush into any long term contracts with foreign firms, but keep the oil in ultimate control of the state.[53]

---

[48] Muttitt, G. (2006). Production Sharing Agreements - Mortgaging Iraq's Oil Wealth. Arab Studies Quarterly, 28(3,4).p.4

[49] Muttitt, G. (2006). Production Sharing Agreements - Mortgaging Iraq's Oil Wealth. Arab Studies Quarterly, 28(3,4).p.4
[50] Muttitt, G. (2006). Production Sharing Agreements - Mortgaging Iraq's Oil Wealth. Arab Studies Quarterly, 28(3,4).p.2

[51] To compare the systems in Kurdistan region and Iraq see: Weisflog, C. (2014, 06 11). Die verhinderte Erdöl-Supermacht. Retrieved 06 11, 2014, from NZZ: http://www.nzz.ch/aktuell/international/auslandnachrichten/schwierige-erdoel-revolution-1.18319688

[52] Muttitt, G. (2006). Production Sharing Agreements - Mortgaging Iraq's Oil Wealth. Arab Studies Quarterly, 28(3,4).p.4

[53] To read more about the reasons why Iraq should keep oil in control of the state see: Muttitt, G. (2006). Production Sharing Agreements - Mortgaging Iraq's Oil Wealth. Arab Studies Quarterly, 28(3,4) and Mahdi, K. (2007). Iraq's Oil Law: Parsing the Fine Print. World Policy Journal, 24(2), 11-23. http://www.jstor.org/stable/40210087

In the case of production sharing agreements international oil companies should have to invest in Iraq (Infrastructure, Education, Training, etc.) and in return be provided with legal security.

Conclusion

Iraq's economic situation enjoys economic growth, government revenue from oil and gas exports, a positive trade balance and relatively low inflation. However channeling oil and gas revenues to lead the charge in generating non-oil based growth is of paramount importance to make the Iraqi economy sustainable in a long run and finally overcoming the resource curse. This implies investments that support economic diversification as a key driver of economic activity through the creation of an enabling environment and investments that remove the binding constraints to growth.

While international oil prices remain high, action must be taken. The Iraqi Government still has sufficient fiscal resources to create the incentives to diversify the economy and create the base for future stable growth.

The public sector has to be shrunk, in order to minimize recurrent spending. However since the large public sector still is the main guarantor of stability, the only way to able to decrease the public sector will be to create employment in the private sector. Therefore incentives to start a business must be created. More transparent and efficient mechanisms for the issuing of permits and licenses must be established.

The already growing access to loans should be increased further. Large foreign investors, like oil companies should have to invest in Iraqi infrastructure and human capital, in return for a clearer legal status.

Investments should be driven by strategic priorities and not by the drive to maintain power.

The Report of US AID summarized as follows: "Critical to long-term success will be making sure that the spoils of higher oil prices are not squandered, or that a positive fiscal balance does not inhibit reforms, but rather that the government embraces change now as a necessity to guarantee future prosperity." [54]

---

[54] United States Agency - International Development. (2012). USAID-TIJARA PROVINCIAL ECONOMIC GROWTH PROGRAM. New York: Report for Prime Minister's Advisory Commission (PMAC). p.10

Bibliography

Bjorvatn, K., Farzanegan, M. R., & Schneider, F. (2012, 7 0). Resource Curse and Power Balance: Evidence from Oil-Rich Countries. *World Development, 40*, 1308--1316.

Blanchard, C. M. (2010). *Iraq: Oil and Gas Sector, Revenue Sharing and U.S. Policy.* Washington: Congressional Research Service.

Boschini, A., Pettersson, J., & Roine, J. (2013, 3 0). The Resource Curse and its Potential Reversal. *World Development, 43*, 19--41.

Devarajan, S., Raballand, G., & Le, T. (2011). Direct Redistribution, Taxation, and Accountability in Oil-Rich Economies: A Proposal. *Center for Global Development Working Paper*.

Donovan, T. W. (2010). *Iraq's Petroleum Industry: Unsettled Issues.* Washington D.C.: Middle East Institute.

Foote, C., Block, W., Crane, K., & Gray, S. (2004). Economic policy and prospects in Iraq. *The Journal of Economic Perspectives, 18*, 47--70.

Frankel, J. (2010). The Natural Resource Curse: A Survey. *HKS Faculty Research Working Paper Series*, 1-45.

Hsieh, C.-T., & Moretti, E. (2006). Did Iraq Cheat the United Nations? Underpricing, Bribes, and the Oil for Food Program. *The Quarterly Journal of Economics, 121*, 1211-1248.

Humphreys, M., Sachs, J., & Stiglitz, J. E. (2007). *Escaping the resource curse.* Cambridge Univ Press.

Mahdi, K. (2007). Iraq's Oil Law: Parsing the Fine Print. *World Policy Journal, 24*(2), 11-23.

Mehlum, H., Moene, K., & Torvik, R. (2006). Institutions and the resource curse*. *The Economic Journal, 116*, 1--20.

Muttitt, G. (2006). Production Sharing Agreements - Mortgaging Iraq's Oil Wealth. *Arab Studies Quarterly, 28*(3,4).

Myers, K. (2012, May 9). *Iraq Revenue Watch.* Retrieved May 14, 2014, from Oil, Power and Democracy in Iraq: Can They Be Reconciled?: http://www.iraqrevenuewatch.org/news/oil-power-and-democracy-iraq-can-they-be-reconciled

Oxford Research International. (2004). *National Survey of Iraq: February 2004.* Oxford.

Robertson, C. (2008, August 10). *The New York Times.* Retrieved April 23, 2014, from Iraq Private Sector Falters; Rolls of Government Soar:

http://www.nytimes.com/2008/08/11/world/middleeast/11baghdad.html?pagewa nted=all

United Nations, World Bank. (2003). *Joint Iraq Needs Assessment: Investment Climate*. New York: UN.

United States Agency - International Development. (2012). *USAID-TIJARA PROVINCIAL ECONOMIC GROWTH PROGRAM*. New York: Report for Prime Minister's Advisory Commission (PMAC).

United States Agency for International Development. (2012). *IRAQ USAID-TIJARA 2012 - PROMOTING JOB CREATION, BUSINESS EXPANSION & ACCESS TO FINANCE*. Washington: PROVINCIAL ECONOMIC GROWTH PROGRAM .

US Energy Information Administration. (2009). *Country Analysis Brief: Iraq*. Washington.

Weisflog, C. (2014, 06 11). *Die verhinderte Erdöl-Supermacht*. Retrieved 06 11, 2014, from NZZ: http://www.nzz.ch/aktuell/international/auslandnachrichten/schwierige-erdoel-revolution-1.18319688

World Bank Group. (2014). *Doing Business Report 2014*. Washington D.C.: World Bank Group.

www.ingramcontent.com/pod-product-compliance
Lightning Source LLC
Chambersburg PA
CBHW021937220326
41598CB00061BA/1605